Super Snake

Gregg Dreise

LEADING PUBLISHER OF ABORIGINAL AND TORRES STRAIT ISLANDER STORYTELLERS.

CHANGING THE WORLD, ONE STORY AT A TIME.

First published 2024. Reprinted in 2026.

Magabala Books Aboriginal Corporation
1 Bagot Street, Broome, Western Australia
Website: www.magabala.com
Email: sales@magabala.com

Magabala Books is assisted by the Australian Government through Creative Australia, its principal arts investment and advisory body, and publishes with support from the WA Government.

Magabala Books is Australia's leading independent Aboriginal and Torres Strait Islander publishing house. We acknowledge the Traditional Owners of the Country on which we live and work. We recognise the unbroken connection to traditional lands, waters and cultures. Through what we publish, we honour all our Elders, peoples and stories, past, present and future.

The illustrations in this book were created using dry rubbing ochres for the backgrounds, and chalk pastels for the skies. Then they are completed with pencils, acrylic paint and paint pens.

Designed by Danielle Bluff
Edited by Cathie Tasker

Printed in China by Toppan Leefung Printing Ltd

ISBN 978-1-922142-95-5 (Print)

ISBN 978-1-922777-45-4 (ePDF)

A catalogue record for this book is available from the National Library of Australia

To all of the people
who live along the Darling River.
Please, look after it.
Come together. Rise up and share.

Gregg Dreise

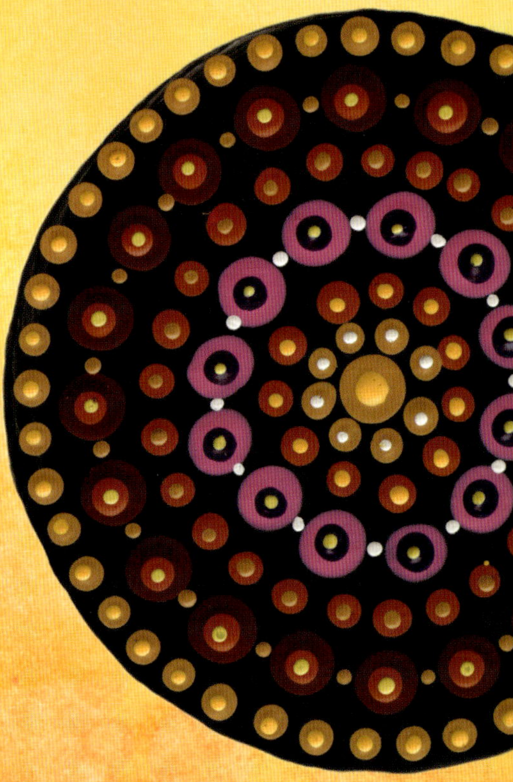

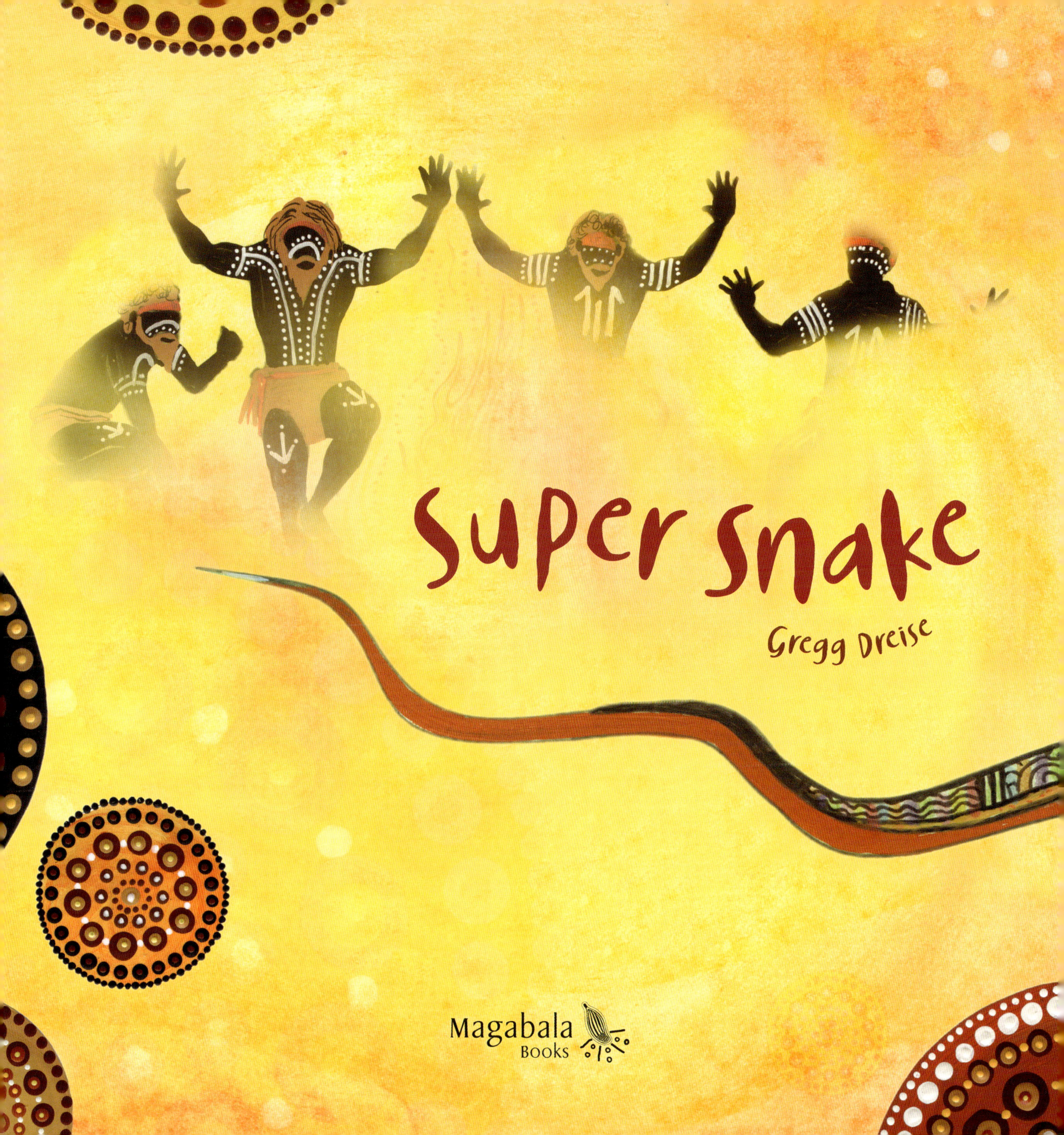

Super Snake

Gregg Dreise

Magabala Books

Way back before
Once-upon-a-time time,
there was the Dreamtime
and the bush was in the
middle of a drought.

Rising waves of heat dried up
every drop of morning dew.

A storm twirled and whirled
above the sunburnt land.
Lightning danced across the ridges
and the sky was ablaze with colour.

One large rainbow curved down.
What a dazzling display from Father Sky!

An enormous creature,
Mundegutta Gooriya the Super Snake,
slithered down that rainbow onto the earth.

He went straight to the Euahlayi Elders
and said he could help them find water.

The Elders tried to be brave
but they were terrified by the great size
and power of the Super Snake.

'Actions speak louder than words!'
Mundegutta Gooriya shouted.

He invited Elders
from different clan groups
to ride on his back.

He took off east.

That Super Snake went fast.
He left Euahlayi Country, through Goomelroi
and entered Ngarabal Country.

They feasted on damper made from Bunya-Bunya
and more Elders climbed on his back.

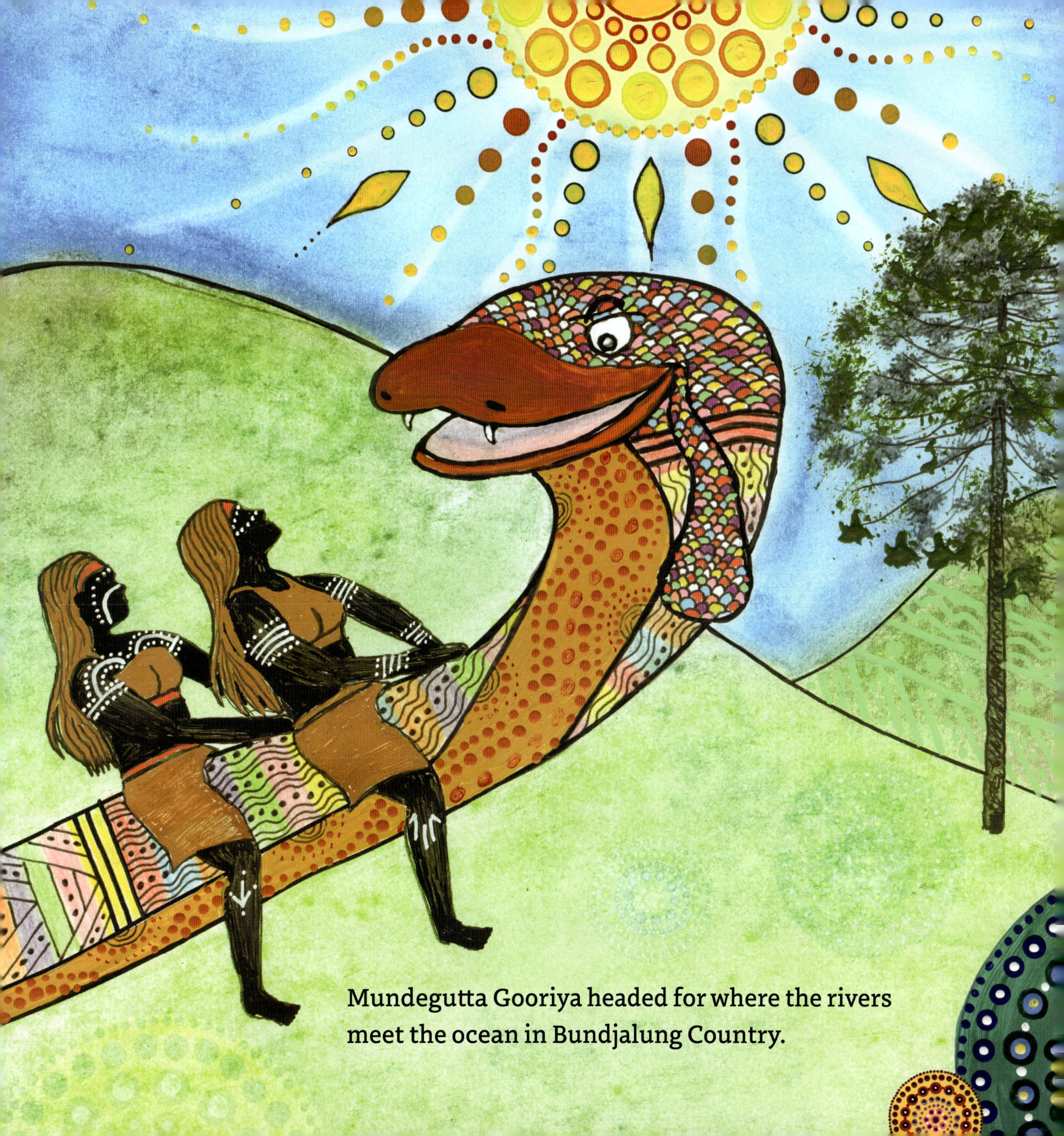

Mundegutta Gooriya headed for where the rivers meet the ocean in Bundjalung Country.

While they feasted on macadamia,
Mundegutta Gooriya taught the Elders how
Yirray, the sun, sucked up the ocean water
to the clouds and left the salt behind.

'Just like the food we are all eating,' he said.
'Water needs to be shared.'

That Super Snake called out,
'You can't have a rainbow without water.'

'Dhurraluwi guuma-li – Come together!
Wantima – Rise up!
Woorri – Share.'

Mundegutta Gooriya took the Elders
to a hilltop in Ngarabal Country.

That Super Snake called out,
'You can't have a rainbow without water.'

'Dhurraluwi guuma-li – Come together!
Wantima – Rise up! Woorri – Share.'

‘Watch me,’ Mundegutta Gooriya said and carved out a river with his strong body.

That river carried the abundant rainwater
from Bundjalung Country north-west
into Barunggam Country.

Then west into Mandandanji Country, and then south into Kooma and then back to Bigambul, Euahlayi and Goomelroi Country.

As the people of the dry west celebrated, he flowed that river into many other countries until he neared the ocean of South Australia.

Tired and sore from creating the rivers,
he lay down to massage away his aches.

That's how he created their
Great Lakes beside the ocean.

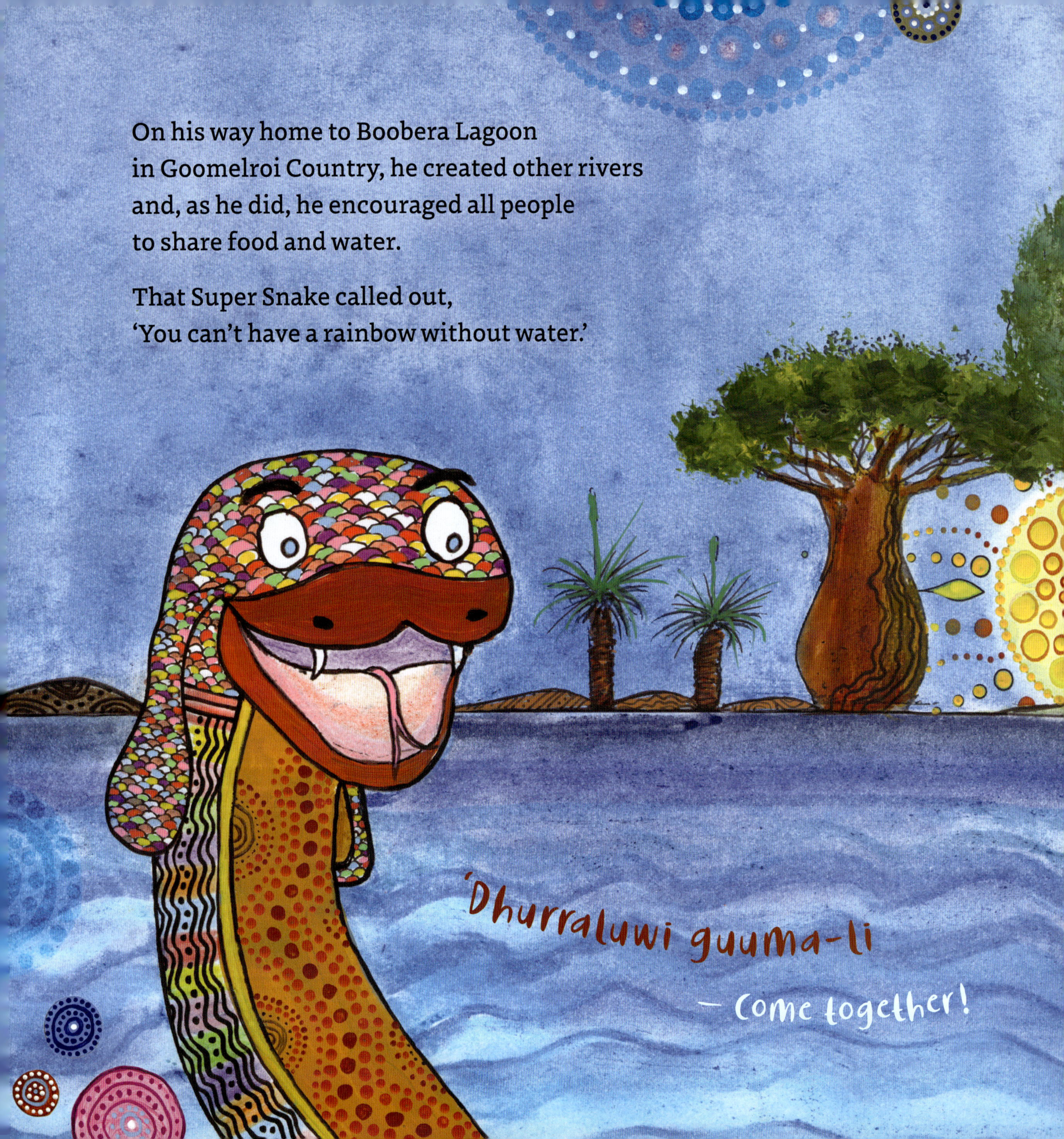

On his way home to Boobera Lagoon in Goomelroi Country, he created other rivers and, as he did, he encouraged all people to share food and water.

That Super Snake called out, 'You can't have a rainbow without water.'

Wantima – Rise up!
Woorri – Share.'

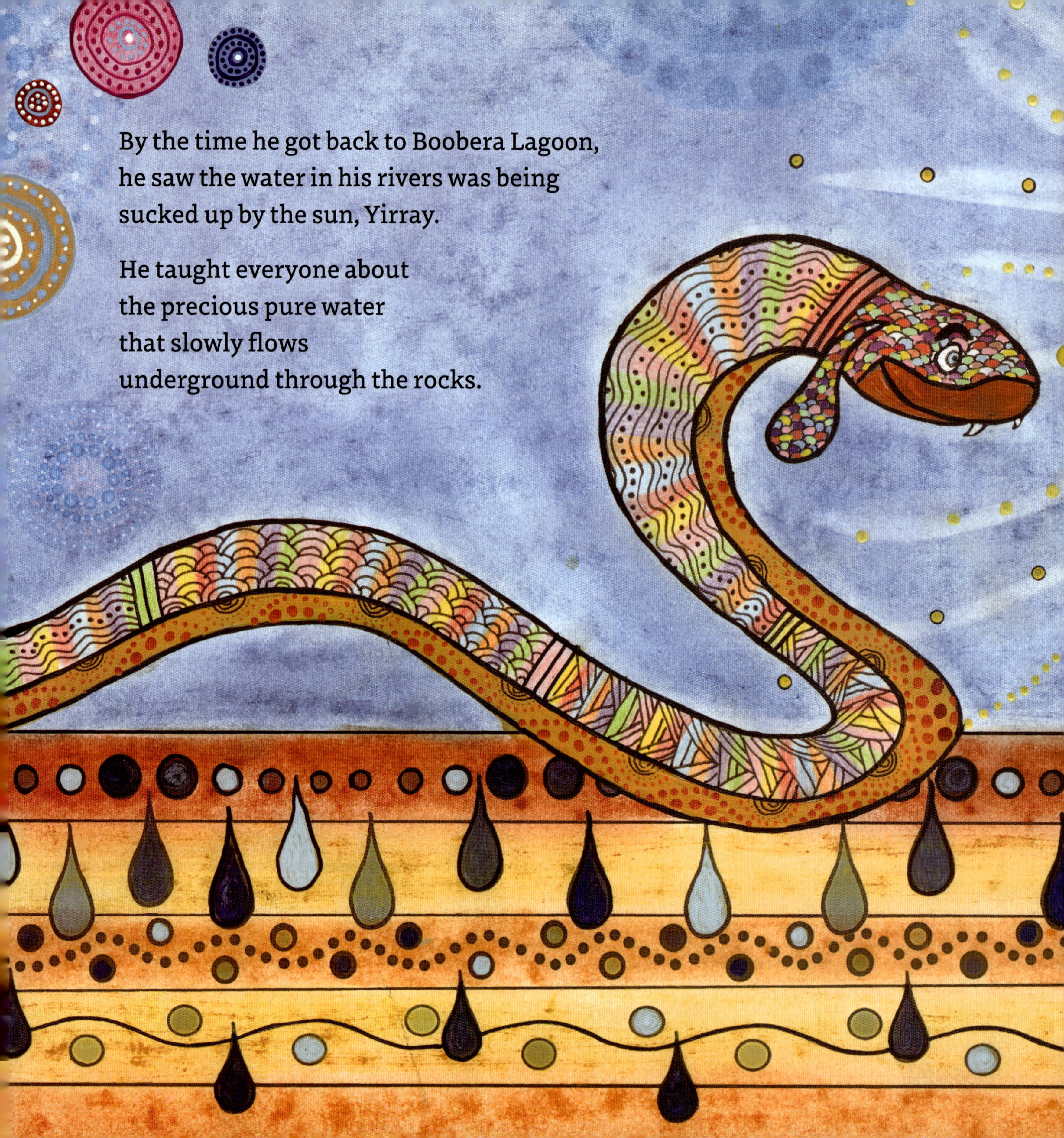

By the time he got back to Boobera Lagoon, he saw the water in his rivers was being sucked up by the sun, Yirray.

He taught everyone about
the precious pure water
that slowly flows
underground through the rocks.

Summoning all his strength,
he thrust his sleek body down
to the underground water system.

He created rock wells at the springs.
'These toowoomba, rock wells,
are always filled with water.

That Super Snake called out,
'You can't have a rainbow without water.'

'Dhurraluwi guuma-li
— Come together!
Wantima — Rise up!
Woorri — Share!'

The people rejoiced in his wisdom
and in his might.

That Super Snake who came down
to earth on a rainbow became aware
of the bad that came with his good.

Every time he bored and drilled down
into the earth, the bad spirits, the Wiranuns,
sang to him and sometimes he listened.

That is why you will hear
both good and bad stories
from around Australia about him.

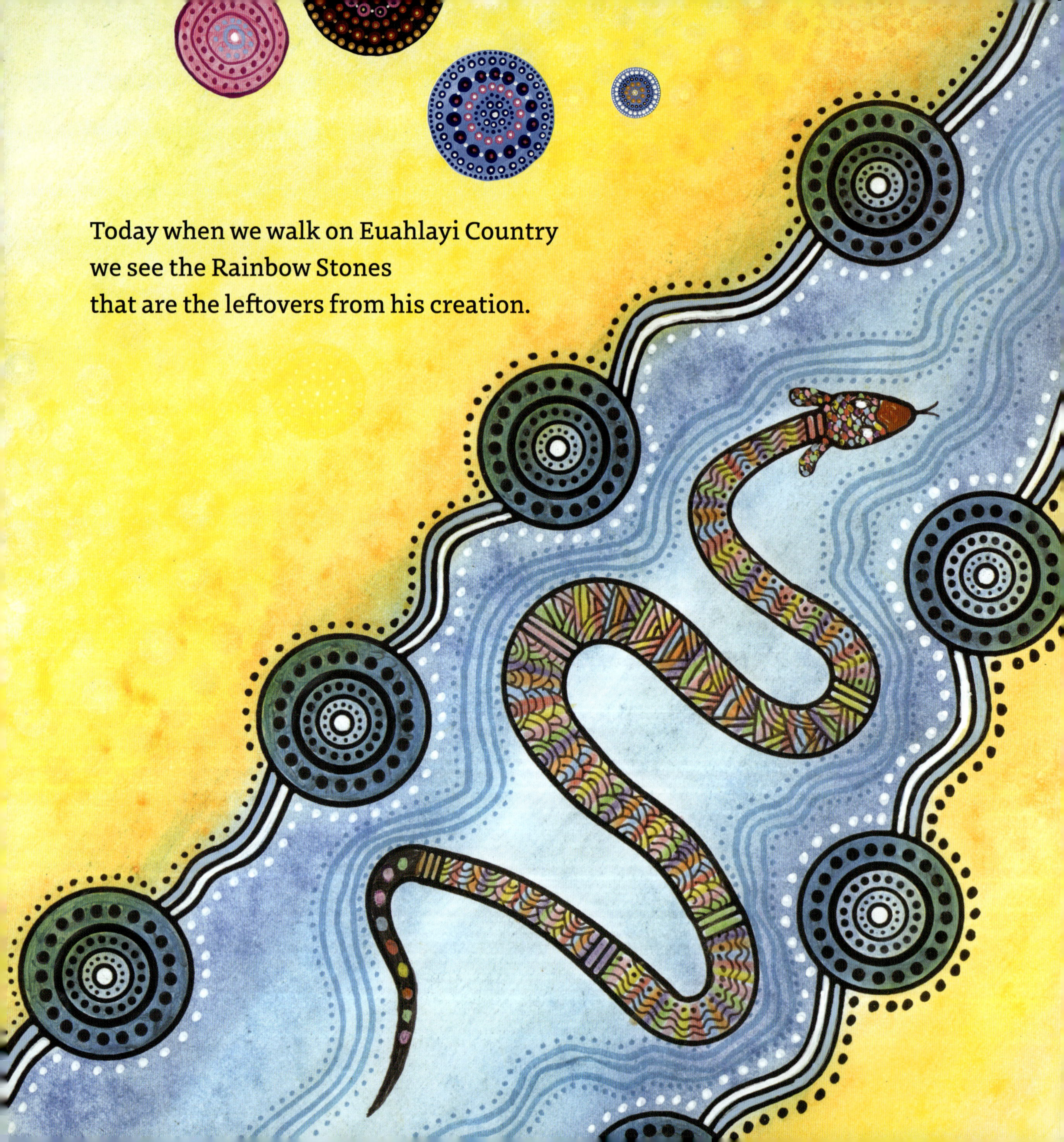

Today when we walk on Euahlayi Country
we see the Rainbow Stones
that are the leftovers from his creation.

And when we visit Goomelroi Country,
but not go into Boobera Lagoon for Ceremony,
we are reminded that this
is the resting place of Mundegutta Gooriya.

We are reminded that we all have good and bad,
so listen to the good.

Come together.

Rise up.

Share.

'Dhurraluwi guuma-li. Wantima. Woorri.'

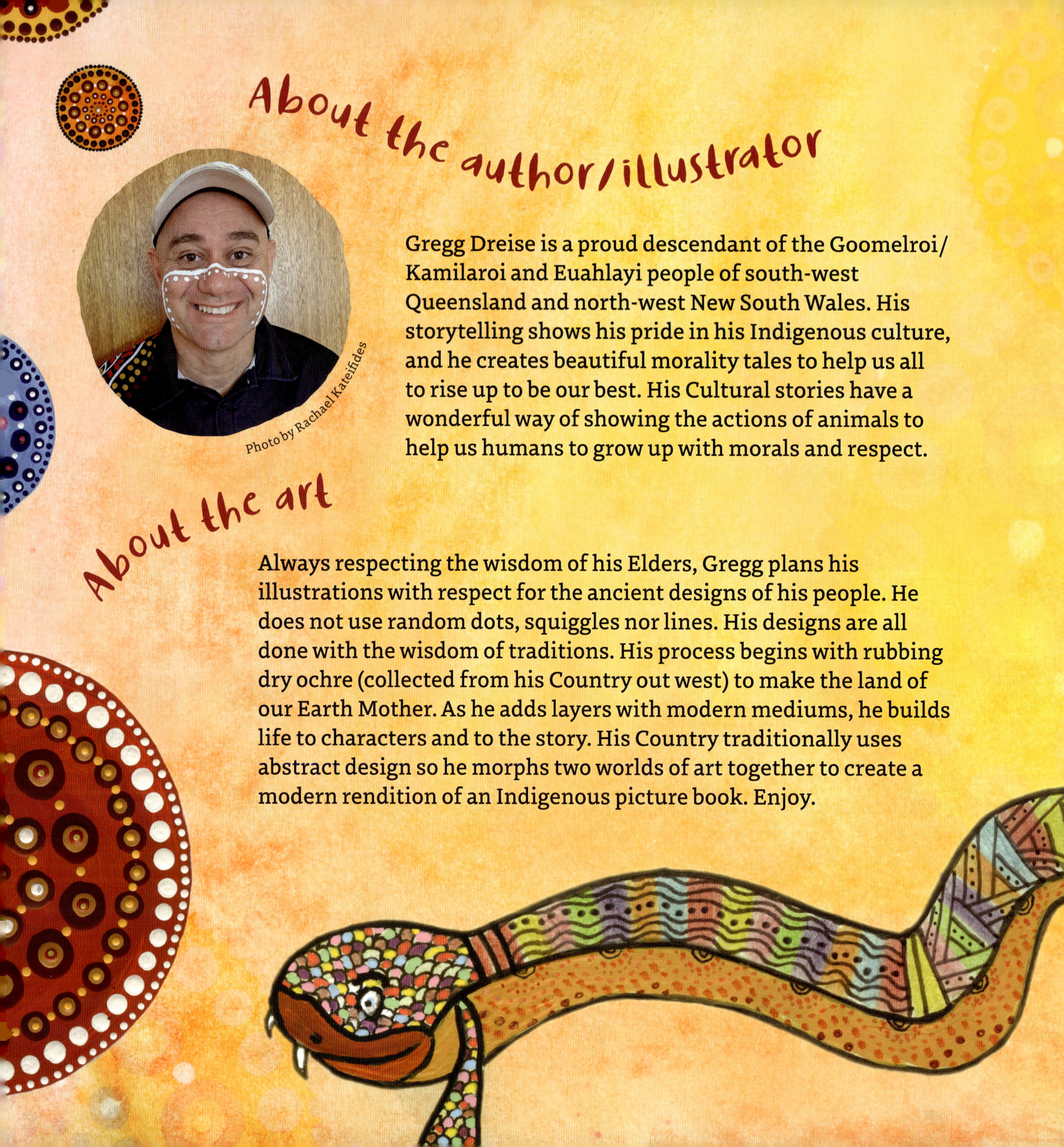

About the author/illustrator

Photo by Rachael Kateifides

Gregg Dreise is a proud descendant of the Goomelroi/ Kamilaroi and Euahlayi people of south-west Queensland and north-west New South Wales. His storytelling shows his pride in his Indigenous culture, and he creates beautiful morality tales to help us all to rise up to be our best. His Cultural stories have a wonderful way of showing the actions of animals to help us humans to grow up with morals and respect.

About the art

Always respecting the wisdom of his Elders, Gregg plans his illustrations with respect for the ancient designs of his people. He does not use random dots, squiggles nor lines. His designs are all done with the wisdom of traditions. His process begins with rubbing dry ochre (collected from his Country out west) to make the land of our Earth Mother. As he adds layers with modern mediums, he builds life to characters and to the story. His Country traditionally uses abstract design so he morphs two worlds of art together to create a modern rendition of an Indigenous picture book. Enjoy.

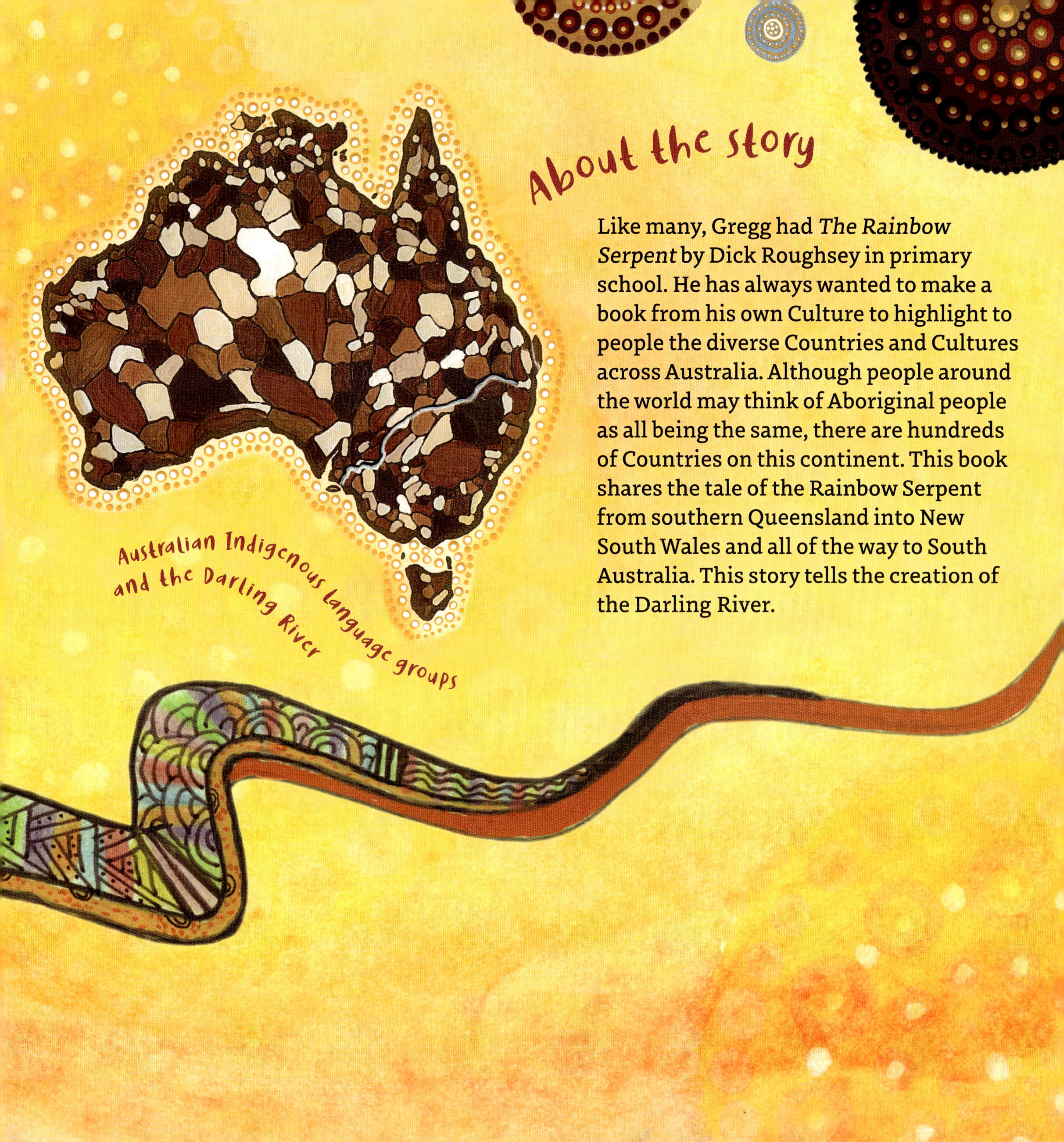

About the story

Like many, Gregg had *The Rainbow Serpent* by Dick Roughsey in primary school. He has always wanted to make a book from his own Culture to highlight to people the diverse Countries and Cultures across Australia. Although people around the world may think of Aboriginal people as all being the same, there are hundreds of Countries on this continent. This book shares the tale of the Rainbow Serpent from southern Queensland into New South Wales and all of the way to South Australia. This story tells the creation of the Darling River.